# LOVE OF GOD

John James Nicolas

ISBN 978-93-5458-920-1
© John James Nicolas 2021
Published in India 2021 by Pencil

*A brand of*

One Point Six Technologies Pvt. Ltd.
123, Building J2, Shram Seva Premises,
Wadala Truck Terminal, Wadala (E)
Mumbai 400037, Maharashtra, INDIA
**E** connect@thepencilapp.com
**W** www.thepencilapp.com



DISCLAIMER: *The opinions expressed in this book are those of the authors and do not purport to reflect the views of the Publisher.*

# Author biography

hi , my name is john nicolas , I am from INDIA ( pune ) , I am spiritual writer  I am born christian , I like to read Bible and I undestood that god is so loving for manking.I like to spend my time in reading and praying..As we grow older our perspective changes towards the life.we became more mature in our life ..everything will vanish in this physical life but **LOVE OF GOD** will remain forever . and we will be in heaven with jesus forever .whatever I got from the Lord I am giving to you...thx jesus..love you jesus..

**john james nicolas**

# CONTENTS

# LOOK AT THE CROSS

one day I was walking on the street of pune its in India.. I was hungry .. I was thursty ..and my shoes was broken from one side and rain started so I sat down one corner of the road and filling very empty . I was looking people while going on their bikes they are happy ,they have everything ..but I was broken person i didint had job,no money,broken shoes and above all it was rainning ..and I started crying sitting all alone beside the corner of the road ...beacause my situation was almost dead..I was crying almost 2 hours on that road..and I was talking to the lord father if you are their please help me ..help me oh lord ,because pain is too much which I am carring , I have nothing father and I am sitiing here all alone ,no umbrella ,no shoes ..no money ..no one is their to help me,no one is their to guide me..are you litsning lord ..are you litsning jesus ...father say something to me ...talk to me...help me oh lord.and then I saw cross in slight vision..I saw cross..and looking than cross my pain moving out from my body..because I felt my pain is nothing front of lords pain on the cross..and then suddenly divine peace came upon me and I startrd praising GOD , hallelujah the wonders god has done ..I am wondrfully made in the mothers womb thx jesus..thx for this air ..thx for my clothes,,thx for my parent..thx for trees ...thx for colors ...thx for breath you gave..thx for everything ..and I was walking on the road  it was rainning and I was praising and worshiping lord ..and when I came to my room i didnt understand ..

one thing I have to tell you ..if you are going through some tough situation dont worry look at the cross ..because jesus took all your pain on the cross.

look at the cross..and tell jesus I love you lord.

# HUG TO FATHER

when we hug each other we show our love to them . when soldier come to home after many years to his house what wife do? she runs toward him ..and embrassed him with hug and she cry she give him kisses ..because her love came back to home..remember the story in the bible about prodigal son what he does when he remember his father love ..then he think their is lot of food in my father house I am like king their ..and he went back to father house..his father was waiting for him that one day I will see my child..and when both see each other they just hug and started crying ..

everyone do mistake in their life but when we remember our heavenly father and we cry front of him ..he gives us genuine ..loving hug ..tell our father that...father I did mistake I commited wrong things in your eyes ..forgive my sins lord ..clean me ...wash my sins with you blood ..jesus come into my life..I welcome you ...hug me lord ..love me lord..i love you

# FORGIVENESS IF FIRST STEP TOWARD SELF DELIVERANCE

Then Jesus said, **"Father, forgive them, for they  do  not know what they    are    doing."** And they    divided up His garments by casting lots. **luke 23:34**.

jesus was pure and holy still people did wrong things against him..but he forgive them its totally fatherly act..father do same thing if child did some mistake father forgives them..and never remember those mistakes...same thing when we love each other **forgive**them . I know it is very difficult but our heavenly father thinks that he is perfect so we should be perfect .

it was very difficult to me when people done wrong thing against me ..and lord was telling me to **forgive**them..I said no father I will not forgive them, why I should forgive them even they did wrong against me..he said **forgive**them ..I said **no..** he said ..**forgive..**whole night talk was going on ..and I was cying and I said lord ..**if you forgive me on the cross ..I forgive them..** after that I felt divine peace is coming upon me..and I felt relax ..calm as I thought i became free person. same way if you are holding grudge in your mind about some one I tell you ..forgive him..because it will be self deliverance for you

**prayer for deliverance** -Father whoever reading this book forgive them as you forgive everyone on the cross wash away thier sins ,clean them with your blood.give them strength to **forgive ,** heal their mind ..body and soul..in jesus mighty name ..amen ( say amen and recieve your healing )

# COMPASSION FOR PEOPLE

**Jesus Feeds the Five Thousand :**10 When the apostles returned, they reported to Jesus what they had done. Then he took them with him and they withdrew by themselves to a town called Bethsaida, 11 but the crowds learned about it and followed him. He welcomed them and spoke to them about the kingdom of God, and healed those who needed healing.12 Late in the afternoon the Twelve came to him and said, "Send the crowd away so they can go to the surrounding villages and countryside and find food and lodging, because we are in a remote place here."13 He replied, "You give them something to eat."They answered, "We have only five loaves of bread and two fish—unless we go and buy food for all this crowd." 14 (About five thousand men were there.)But he said to his disciples, "Have them sit down in groups of about fifty each." 15 The disciples did so, and everyone sat down. 16 Taking the five loaves and the two fish and looking up to heaven, he gave thanks and broke them. Then he gave them to the disciples to distribute to the people. 17 They all ate and were satisfied, and the disciples picked up twelve basketfuls of broken pieces that were left over. **luke 9 : 10-17**

if will see above story in the bible jesus is compassionate about people ,bible says GOD IS LOVE **1st john 4 : 16.** when we show compassion to other people we fullfill gods desire in our life . because he is love he has compassion for people ,he thinks everyone should get eternal life..everyone should get **salvation** through **jesus..**

**whatever you did for one of the least of these brothers and sisters of mine**

40 "The King will reply, 'Truly I tell you, whatever you did for one of the least of these brothers and sisters of mine, you did for me.'

41 "Then he will say to those on his left, 'Depart from me, you who are cursed, into the eternal fire prepared for the devil and his angels. 42 For I was hungry and you gave me nothing to eat, I was thirsty and you gave me nothing to drink, 43 I was a stranger and you did not invite me in, I needed clothes and you did not clothe me, I was sick and in prison and you did not look after me.'

44 "They also will answer, 'Lord, when did we see you hungry or thirsty or a stranger or needing clothes or sick or in prison, and did not help you?'

45 "He will reply, 'Truly I tell you, whatever you did not do for one of the least of these, you did not do for me.'**Matthew 25:40-45**

sometimes we are desperetly need of something not only money matters but many other thing ...and then only someone help us we fill love about that person...if you are looking somewong hungry ..feed him...someone thirsty...give him water..if you are capable to do something for people do it ..because thats what god expect from you...give love..recieve love..freely you get ...freely you give

# GIVE THANKS FOR EVERYTHING YOU HAVE

**GOD is creator of everything**

1 In the beginning was the Word, and the Word was with God, and the Word was God. 2 The same was in the beginning with God.3 All things were made by him; and without him was not any thing made that was made. **john 1 : 1-3** .

whatever we are looking in the world everything is created by Lord **JESUS CHRIST..** he is craetor of everything ..withought him was not anything made that was made.. he made heaven and earth give glory and thx to him , he made galaxies give honour to him , he made animals,trees,flowers,hills and mountains,birds ..everything he made..he is greater than we think...words are short to him for praise ..his name is above all name ..his name has authority above everything...his name is **JESUS CHRIST SON OF GOD.**

Give thx when you wokeup in morning ..jesus I am giving you thx for this beautiful day ...thx for my family..thx for my parents,thx for my child..thx for my work..thx for my clothes..thx for air I am breathing..thx for **holy spirit ,** thx for wisdom you gave me ..thx for all trees..thx for my food

..thx for understanding..thx for my house..thx for my car..thx for joy you gave me.hallelujah glory to almighty **GOD**

even in difficult situation we should give thx to the lord ,not even good situation but in difficult situation we should praise and thanks lord

you know the song - **Give thx with greatful heart**

Give thanks with a grateful heartGive thanks to the Holy OneGive thanks because He's given Jesus Christ, His Son

Give thanks with a grateful heartGive thanks to the Holy OneGive thanks because He's given Jesus Christ, His Son

And now let the weak say, "I am strong"Let the poor say, "I am richBecause of what the Lord has done for us"...give thx

# SALVATION IS GREATEST GIFT

yes their is eternal life after this life..everyone wants to be in heaven ..heaven is very beautiful place ..beautiful garden ..flowers ..gods river..and wonderful music beyond our imagination..yes their is beautiful life with jesus after this life...because our heavenly father have wonderful plans for his children...

how we will get salvation ? ..through **jesus christ** yes because bible says

 6 Jesus answered, "I am the way and the truth and the life. No one comes to the Father except through me. **john 14:6**

9 If you declare with your mouth, "Jesus is Lord," and believe in your heart that God raised him from the dead, you will be saved. 10 For it is with your heart that you believe and are justified, and it is with your mouth that you profess your faith and are saved. 11 As Scripture says, "Anyone who believes in him will never be put to shame. 12 For there is no difference between Jew and Gentile—the same Lord is Lord of all and richly blesses all

who call on him, 13 for, "Everyone who calls on the name of the Lord will be saved." **Romans 10 : 9 -13**

when you declare with your mouth that **jesus is lord ,** you open door for jesus to come in heart .and after that you got saved .its invitation to god in your heart

**salvation prayer -** father I come near to you , jesus forgive my sins clean me with your blood , you died for me on the cross and risen on 3rd day now you are in heaven , jesus I boldly declare and confess that your are my Lord and my saviour .come into my heart lord ,thx for my salvation ,now I am new person in you.

# YOUR TIME WITH LORD

God is person ,talk to him personaly,as two person are talking to each other, spend quality time with him ,meance you have to adore him , adore him for his creation , give him thx for everything you have.

**personal prayer**-6 But whenever you pray, go into your room and shut the door and pray to your Father who is in secret; and your Father who sees in secret will reward you. 7 'When you are praying, do not heap up empty phrases as the Gentiles do; for 6 they think that they will be heard because of their many words.  **matthew 6 : 6-7**

bible tells us about personal time with lord, just go to quite place, remove your worries from mind and start adoring lord ,magnify him ,make him real person in your life, and he is there for love you ,he is there for hug you ,he is there to guide you,he is good counselor and comforter,.Go deeper and more deeper with his relation as he is our father..while praying you can keep some background worship music ( soaking in presence music ) ,because music create wondurful atmosphere around us .and God love music .try to create good atmosphere around you.

praise and worship lord jesus adore him and as you go deeper with him in prayer you can tell him about your need ( he knows what you want )

**prayer in group-** 19 "Again, truly I tell you that if two of you on earth agree about anything they ask for, it will be done for them by my Father in heaven. 20 For where two or three gather in my name, there am I with them." **matthew 18: 19 - 20.**

when two person agree about one thing and they  will ask Lord and according to will of god that thing is good in god eyes ,he will  provide  you  that  thing..Attending  church service is important because together we worship and pray to lord.

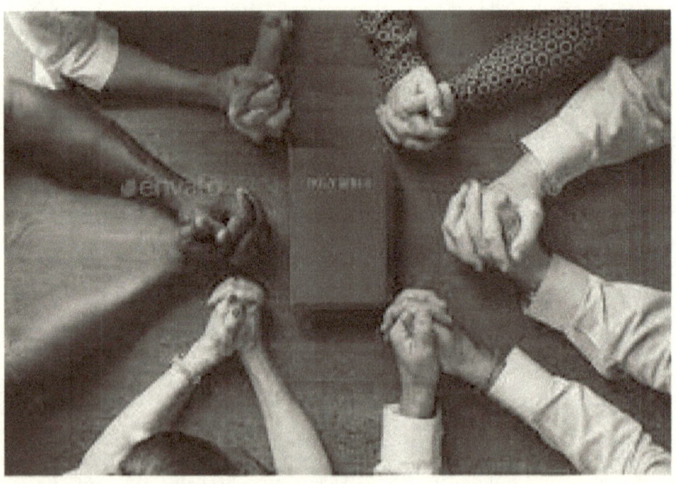

# LOVE OF GOD

And we have known and believed the love that God has for us. God is love, and he who abides in love abides in God, and God in him. 1st john 4 :16who is in love he is abide in God ,so love of god is first principle thing,remember the love of cross  what Jesus done for us on the cross.God is love he is complete being with love,he is ocean of Love ,as god love us we should love each other.For God so loved the world, that he gave his only begotten Son, that whoever believes in him should not perish, but have everlasting life. **john 3:16**

 love is patient and is kind; love doesn't envy. Love doesn't brag, is not proud, doesn't behave itself inappropriately, doesn't seek its own way, is not provoked, takes no account of evil; doesn't rejoice in unrighteousness, but rejoices with the truth; bears all things, believes all things, hopes all things, endures all things. Love never fails. **1 Corinthians 13:4-8**

13 And now these three remain: faith, hope and love. But the greatest of these is love.1 Corinthians 13 :13 .  love of god should be the foundation of person lifewhat is love of God - 23 Jesus replied, "Anyone who loves me will obey my teaching. My Father will love them, and we will come to them and make our home with them. **John 14:23**

**Love of God** is personal experience with him,pray god that he shuld fill you with his love..give me your loving experience..send your love rain on me..God forgive me..I ask forgiveness to those whom I heart..keep me in your love.


**prayer for you**- Dear father I come to your presence .I pray for my beloved brother/sister ..Jesus fill them with your love..Give them your heart.. so they will undestand your will in their life..have mercy upon them..fill them with your **Agape Love**..

LOVE YOU
JESUS
WITH ALL MY HEART

# BLESSING FROM BIBLE

Isaac planted crops in that land and the same year reaped a hundredfold, because  the Lord blessed  him. 13 The  man became rich, and his wealth continued to grow until he became  very  wealthy. **Genesis  26:12-13** isaac  panted crops and he reaped hundredfold . when god is with you whatever you will you will prosper. I pray to god that whoever reading this now god bless them abundantly..

And you shall remember the Lord your God, for it is He who gives you power to get wealth, that He may establish His covenant which He swore to your fathers, as it is this day.**Deuteronomy 8:18 ,** God give us the power to get wealth ,pray to God that ..God give me your Divine knowledge Understanding to get wealth.so me and my family will glorify you ..bless my family lord ..give me abundence..

**Blessings for Obedience**

 If  you  fully  obey  the Lord your  God  and  carefully follow all  his  commands I  give  you  today, the Lord your

God will set you high above all the nations on earth. 2 All these blessings will come on you and accompany you if you obey the Lord your God 3 You will be blessed in the city and blessed in the country.4 The fruit of your womb will be blessed, and the crops of your land and the young of your livestock—the calves of your herds and the lambs of your flocks.5 Your basket and your kneading trough will be blessed.6 You will be blessed when you come in and blessed when you go out.7 The Lord will grant that the enemies who rise up against you will be defeated before you. They will come at you from one direction but flee from you in seven.8 The Lord will send a blessing on your barns and on everything you put your hand to. The Lord your God will bless you in the land he is giving you.9 The Lord will establish you as his holy people, as he promised you on oath, if you keep the commands of the Lord your God and walk in obedience to him. 10 Then all the peoples on earth will see that you are called by the name of the Lord, and they will fear you. 11 The Lord will grant you abundant prosperity—in the fruit of your womb, the young of your livestock and the crops of your ground—in the land he swore to your ancestors to give you.12 The Lord will open the heavens, the storehouse of his bounty, to send rain on your land in season and to bless all the work of your hands. You will lend to many nations but will borrow from none. 13 The Lord will make you the head, not the tail. If you pay attention to the commands of the Lord your God that I give you this day and carefully follow them, you will always be at the top, never at the bottom. 14 Do not turn aside from any of the commands I give you today, to the right or to the left, following other gods and serving them. **Deuteronomy 28:1-14** . declare this blessing in your family and youself ..that you are blessed every area in your life.

Ask me, and I will make the nations your inheritance, the ends of the earth your possession.**Psalm 2 :8** . you can ask nations for inheritance because he is creator of universe ..hallelujah.

Only be strong and very courageous, being careful to do according to all the law that Moses my servant commanded you. Do not turn from it to the right hand or to the left, that you may have good success[a] wherever you go. 8 This Book of the Law shall not depart from your mouth, but you shall meditate on it day and night, so that you may be careful to do according to all that is written in it. For then you will make your way prosperous, and then you will have good success.**Joshua 1:7-8** .

I will give you the treasures of darkness, riches stored in secret places, so that you may know that I am the LORD, the God of Israel, who summons you by name. For the sake of Jacob my servant, of Israel my chosen, I summon you by name and bestow on you a title of honor, though you do not acknowledge me.

**Isaiah 45 :3**

## Glory of zion

Arise, shine; for your light has come, and the glory of the Lord has risen upon you. 2For darkness shall cover the earth, and thick darkness the peoples; but the Lord will arise upon you, and his glory will appear over you. 3Nations shall come to your light, and kings to the brightness of your dawn. 4Lift up your eyes and look around; they all gather together, they come to you; your sons shall come from far away, and your daughters shall be carried on their nurses' arms. 5Then you shall see and be radiant; your heart shall thrill and rejoice, because the abundance of the sea shall be brought to you, the wealth of the nations shall come to you. 6A multitude of camels shall cover you, the young camels of Midian and Ephah; all those from Sheba shall come. They shall bring gold and frankincense, and shall proclaim the praise of the Lord. 7All the flocks of Kedar shall be gathered to you, the rams of Nebaioth shall minister to you; they shall be acceptable on my altar, and I will glorify my glorious house. 8Who are these that fly like a cloud, and like doves to their windows?

9For the coastlands shall wait for me, the ships of Tarshish first, to bring your children from far away, their silver and gold with them, for the name of the Lord your God, and for the Holy One of Israel, because he has glorified you. **Isaiah 60:1-9**

For I will pour water on the thirsty land, and streams on the dry ground;I will pour out my Spirit on your offspring,and my blessing on your descendants.

**Isaiah 44:3  ..** you can declare that jesus I recieve your living water on my life..

## The Priestly Blessing

22 The Lord said to Moses, 23 Tell Aaron and his sons, 'This is how you are to bless the Israelites. Say to them:

24 The Lord bless you and keep you;25 the Lord make his face shine on you  and be gracious to you 26 the Lord turn his face toward you and give you peace.

**Numbers 6:22-27  ..**you can bless your family with this priestly blessings.

**prayer for you -  Lord jesus** me and my brother/sister come to your presence lord bless them mightly in every area of their life ,heal them ,they are blessed in jesus name ...give your divine favour to them ..fullfil their heart desire .they are blessed going out coming in ..their child is blessed..thx for your supernatural provision in their life..thank you father for this wonderful time..in jesus mighty name we prayed ..amen and amen.

# THANKS AND LOVE  YOU

I love you my brother and sister in christ .whoever reading this book **.JESUS** love you so much .you are child of god regarding bible

Yet to all who did receive him, to those who believed in his name, he gave the right to become children of God . **John 1 : 12**

so you are child of god ,this is your authority in christ .you are choosen for kingdome of god **.GOD BLESS YOU , LOVE YOU.**

**I want to give thx to Father**

**I want to give thx to Jesus**

**I want to give thx to holy spirit**

**I want to give thx to you reader. love you ..**

.

**john nicolas**

9 789354 589201